What Do Animals Eat?

Animal Appetite

A
B
C's

Written by Bonnie Banks-Beers
Illustrated by Jonah Reece Beers

Copyright © 2012 Bonnie Banks-Beers
All rights reserved.
ISBN: 1470120682
ISBN: 9781470120689
Library of Congress Control Number: 2012903433
CreateSpace Independent Publishing Platform
North Charleston, South Carolina

About Animals
(A Note on Sources)

Scientific research will continually modify
the animal information in this book,
as the facts in encyclopedias and other
reference sources continually evolve when
new discoveries are made.

As Albert Einstein once said:
"The important thing is not to stop questioning.
Curiosity has its own reason for existing."

Dedication

for Aileen & Caroline, Sierra & Alyssa;
Abigail & Rebecca;
and Sarah.

Acknowledgments

I'd like to acknowledge my mom for planting the seed of inspiration to write a children's book; my dad for reading me bedtime stories on "Lapland" when I was little; my brother for being such a good example as an avid reader when we were growing up together; the many teachers and students and friends and authors who have influenced me over the years; my husband for his technical expertise and boundless encouragement; and my children for their wonder and curiosity of life.

If my son had not persistently asked me the question "What do animals eat?", with its many variations, when he was about four years old, this book would never have come to be.

I'd also like to thank Bill George of Touchstone Theatre for recommending CreateSpace to me as a publisher for my first published book. Special thanks to senior publishing consultant Whitney Parks for answering my many initial questions and to my Design Team for their responsiveness to my vision, thorough communication, and attention to detail throughout the publishing process.

What Do Animals Eat?

Some eat plants and some eat meat.

It depends upon where they do live,

And the teeth and the bodies that Nature did give.

A

Anteaters don't have any teeth,
Just a hole at the end of their snout.
They dine upon meals of ants and termites
With a long, sticky tongue stuck way out.

They live in the grasslands and forests of
America - Central and South.
It is here that they eat their limited diet
With their toothless and long-snouted mouth.

B

Birds are hungry most all of the time.
They need lots of food so they can fly.
For their heart rate and temperature
really do rise
When they exercise up in the sky.

Having no teeth, birds must swallow food whole.
Never try it, or you could choke.
A swallow may swallow 800 mosquitoes
In a single day - that is no joke.

Blue jays that live in a forest eat berries;
From a field, much grain a crow takes;
Penguins, swimming under the water, catch fish;
And desert road runners like snakes.

Crocodiles live where it's hot and it's wet.
They have quite a large appetite.
With a mouthful of sharp teeth they
catch animals
But can't chew after taking a bite.

If the animal's small, they will swallow it whole -
Like a fish or a small water rat.
But if it is big, they will swallow in chunks -
Like a rhino, pig, ox, goat, deer, cat.

D

Deer live in various places:
Hot deserts and cool forests, too.
They eat standing up - grass, twigs, bark,
flowers, leaves -
But barely take time to chew.

In a hurry to get to a safe place
Where they bring back up poorly-chewed food,
The deer chew on cud which they swallow again
Lying down, looking after their brood.

E

Elephants are the largest animals
Who live upon the land.
In African or Asian jungles,
Six to twelve feet tall they stand.

Because they are so very big,
They eat hundreds of pounds of food.
But it must be eaten in several small batches
Or these messy eaters will brood.

Trees are knocked over to eat
the top branches,
And coconuts cracked with their feet.
When water is scarce they dig deep
with their tusks
So they can drink as well as eat.

F

Flamingos live in shallow lagoons
And dine with their heads upside down.
They scoop up their food with their
really bent bills
To find animals all around.

Algae and small water animals - yum!
Snails and insects, too.
And to keep their pink color in captivity,
Shrimp and lobster shells at the zoo.

G

Giraffes are the tallest of animals,
Sometimes 18 feet tip to tip.
They live in the woodlands of Africa,
Gathering food with their tongue and top lip.

Twigs, leaves, and fruit of the bushes and trees
Are the giraffes' most favorite "eats".
Like a cow, they chew cud for a second chewing.
They can go without water for weeks.

Hippos have very big stomachs
And bodies that are thick with fat.
They swim in the lakes and the rivers by day.
Now what can be cooler than that?

At night they come out of the water
To feed upon hay and some grass.
With long, curved front teeth that grow
throughout their lives,
They eat fruits and veggies in mass.

Iguanas who live by the shore
Have a diet of mostly seaweed.
They like to drink saltwater instead of fresh
And dive for some algae to feed.

Iguanas who live in the desert
Are lizards who do not like bugs.
Instead they eat fruit, flowers, and
leaves of plants
And lay eggs in the tunnels they've dug.

Iguanas who live in the rainforest,
Often camouflaged up in the trees,
High dive to swim in the water below,
And also eat fruit, flowers, leaves.

J

Jackals, of Asia and Africa,
Live where lions dwell.
The jackals howl when they spot some food -
It's the lion's dinner bell.

Jackals share the freshly-killed meat
That the lions did hunt (their leftovers).
And then they scavenge for anything else.
They even eat garbage, those rovers!

K

Koala bears live in Australia and
The truth is, a bear they are not.
But like kangaroos with a pouch on their tummy,
They carry their young ones a lot.

Eucalyptus trees provide the leaves
That koalas famously eat.
They like to drink water when they are ill -
And when there is way too much heat.

L

Lions are "kings of the jungle",
Such very big powerful cats.
They don't like thick forests, but woodlands
and plains,
Indian and African flats.

Look out all you hoofed animals!
The lion will have you for dinner.
Deer, antelope, zebras, and others beware -
This hunter is usually a winner.

M

Monkeys like to eat bananas,
'Tis a fact that is very well-known.
But like you and me, they like variety
Of most kinds of fruits and nuts grown.

In addition to fruits they like veggies
And the roots and the leaves of some plants.
They eat smaller jungle animals, too.
Namely, scorpions and ants.

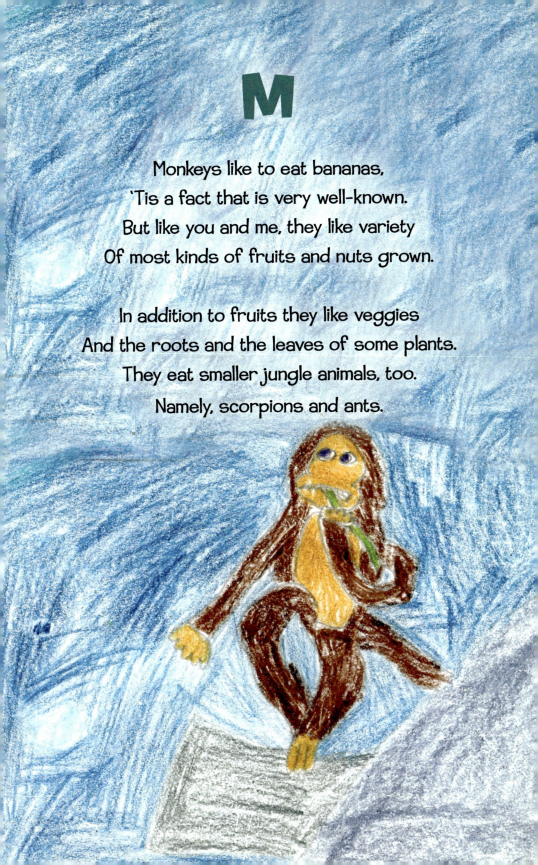

N

Nautilus live in the sea:
South Pacific, Indian Ocean as well.
They have a very soft body
Protected by a spiral shell.

Usually, when they are full-grown
They're the size of a person's fist.
Crabs and other crustaceans are among
Foods on their carrion dinner list.

Octopus live in the ocean
And have eight arms, as you know.
By sucking in lots of salt water,
They spit out to make themselves go.

With suckers on all of their arms,
They reach out for food and they grab,
Putting some lunch in their beak-like mouth -
Perhaps a tasty fish or a crab.

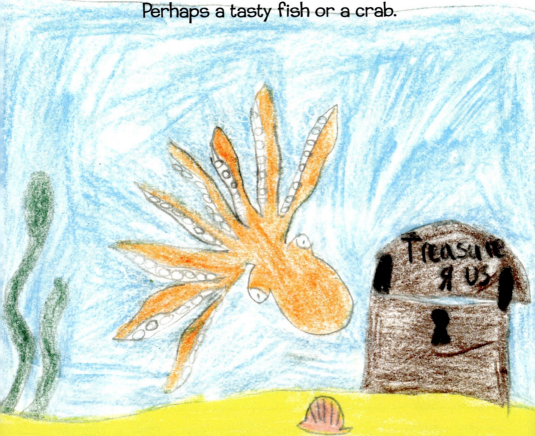

P

Panda bears are not really bears,
But raccoons' distant cousins.
Living in the mountains of China,
They eat bamboo by the dozens.

There are two kinds of pandas:
giant and lesser.
The "giants" eat mostly bamboo.
The "lesser" eat more foods - like fruits,
roots, and eggs,
And carrots when kept in a zoo.

Q

Queen bees are the female bees
With important jobs to bring.
They lay eggs in the honeycomb,
Hatching new honey bees fall and spring.

The queen eats "royal jelly",
A special kind of honey.
In five years' time, one million eggs laid -
More babies than a bunny!

R

Raccoons can be mischievous hunting for food:
They often go where people live,
And remove lids off of folks' garbage cans
To see what food the trash may give.

In the wild, they fish with their fingers
And tend to "wash" food so it's wet.
Like bears, raccoons reach into beehives
For sweet-tasting honey to get.

S

Sharks are eternally hungry,
Known as "scavengers of the sea".
They like to eat animals who have been hurt,
And even eat garbage - it's free!

Their powerful jaws have large teeth
In rows side by side - what a sight.
When sharks lose a tooth, it is quite soon replaced
By another tooth so they can bite.

T

Toads hold the world's fastest record
For capturing food (they are quick):
A fiftieth of a second to stick out their tongue
And pull food in their mouth with a lick.

Their tongue is attached to the front
of their mouth,
Not the back like for you and for me.
It's quick and it's sticky to grab hold of food
Like the insects and fish they do see.

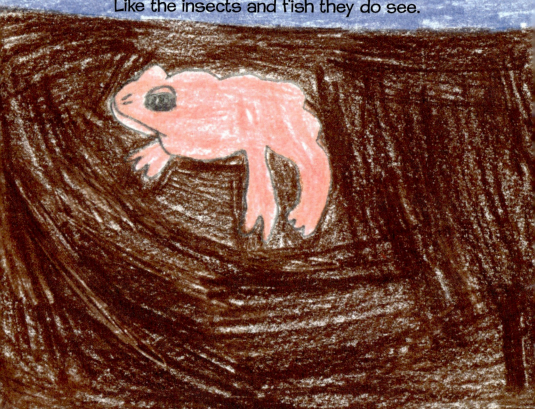

U

Urchins of the sea
Live on the ocean's floor.
Algae and seaweed are favorite foods,
And each other when hungry for more!

They look like spiny plants
With a Pacific or Caribbean home.
Purple, red, green, black or brown -
Don't step on one when you roam.

V

Vultures are odd-looking birds,
With their long crooked necks and bent beaks.
Unlike the hawk who is strong
through-and-through,
They have beaks and feet that are weak.

Because of this weakness they can't
Catch an animal strong and alive.
So they watch and they wait for an animal to die,
And this is the way they survive.

W

Whales are the largest animals
Who live on planet Earth.
Blue whales eat some of the ocean's
tiniest food -
These tiny plankton give the whale great girth.

Blue whales are bigger than dinosaurs were.
A baby's as big as a bus!
Drinking mother's milk, they gain
incredible weight -
200-plus pounds a day - lots more than us.

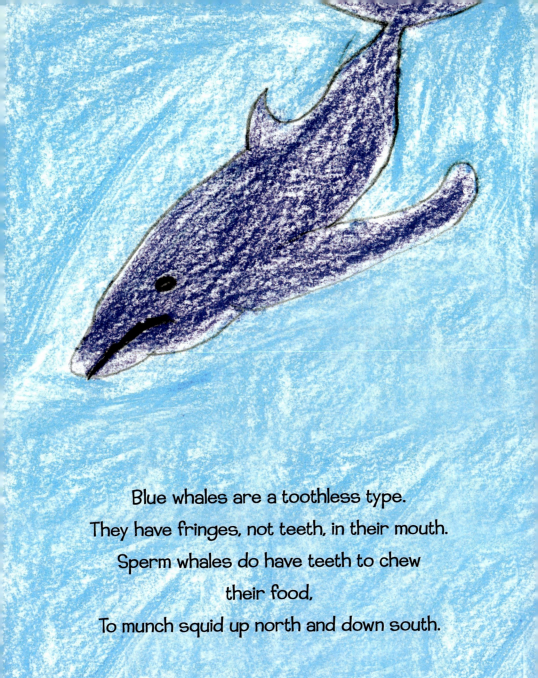

Blue whales are a toothless type.
They have fringes, not teeth, in their mouth.
Sperm whales do have teeth to chew
their food,
To munch squid up north and down south.

X

Xenops are rainforest birds
Who live in the holes of trees.
They gather grass and other plants,
For here their nests will be.

To feed themselves and their young
They use their short, pointed beak.
Hammering branches that are decayed,
Insects like ants they do seek.

Y

Yaks are "grunting oxen" of
The plateaus of Tibet.
Covered with long and silky fur,
Yaks live in the cold - no fret.

A relative of the cow
(The bovine family),
Yak chew their cud from eating grass
And are milked for Tibetan tea.

z

Zebras are horses' cousins
From Africa, south and east.
To hide among the tall grass there are
Black and white stripes on this beast.

Essentially grass eaters,
They drink water quite often, too.
They're known to take "baths" in the sand
and the dirt
And run fast when lions pursue.

People are animals, too.
And what kind of food do we eat?
Many plants: grains, fruits, and vegetables, too,
(And some) also milk, eggs, and meat.

People live all over the world.
Some where it's cold, others hot.
The foods that we favor are really diverse.
Our native foods vary a lot.

If you're wondering what others do eat,
Here's an easy way to take a look:
Instead of traveling all over the world,
Merely open an ethnic cookbook!

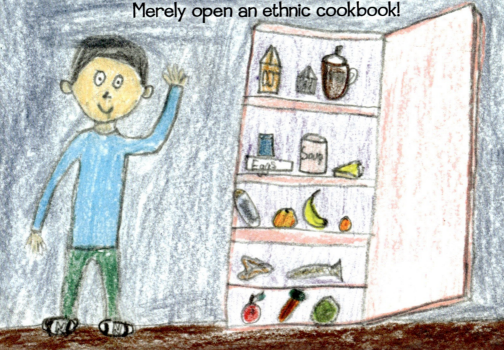

About the Author

Bonnie Banks-Beers finds literary inspiration at the oldest continuously running bookstore in the world - the Moravian Bookshop in Bethlehem, PA - where she currently takes her daughter to story-time, and where she previously worked as head cook and kitchen manager before attending the Natural Gourmet Cookery School in NYC. From time to time, Bonnie has been known to work as a freelance musician and teach kids to play cards (especially Pinochle) in math-related after school workshops. One of her favorite things is to explore farmers' markets and meet interesting people and their local produce. Bonnie resides in the Lehigh Valley, PA.

Contact Bonnie via Facebook.

About the Illustrator

Jonah Beers drew the illustrations for this book while in 6th grade at Saucon Valley Middle School and the book was published while in 8th grade. At the time of publication, he plays the trombone in the concert and jazz bands. He likes drawing pictures and reading. In his free time, Jonah enjoys playing his XBox 360, and likes playing football, basketball, and riding his bike while hanging out with friends. Jonah also likes to watch *SpongeBob SquarePants* and *Good Luck Charlie* on TV. He will eat anything served on his plate as long as it's not moving (within reason).

Proceeds

At the time of this publication, an estimated 1 in 5 children in America battle hunger. Since this is essentially a children's book about eating, we have decided to donate a portion of our revenue from the sales of this book to food-focused charities such as *Share Our Strength*, a national nonprofit that is fighting - and seeking to end - childhood hunger in America. Please join us in this endeavor.

Sincerely, Bonnie and Jonah

Made in the USA
Lexington, KY
25 November 2017